Heart
to
Heart

Heart to Heart

with Kathryn Kuhlman

VOLUME ONE

BL BRIDGE
LOGOS

Newberry, FL 32669

Bridge-Logos

Newberry, FL 32669 USA

Heart to Heart with Kathryn Kuhlman, Volume 1
by Kathryn Kuhlman

Copyright © 1983, 1998
The Kathryn Kuhlman Foundation

Printed in the United States of America.

Library of Congress Catalog Card Number: 98-70939
International Standard Book Number 978-0-88270-750-1

All Scripture quotations are from the *King James Version* of the Bible, unless otherwise indicated.

8-16-16

Contents

Foreword

One of the most popular cassettes offered by Kathryn Kuhlman was the one entitled "The Beginning of Miracles." It was on that tape that she told of her early ministry, her disappointments, the secret of her ministry, and the source of healing power—the Holy Spirit.

Many have written to us requesting printed sermons such as that one. Because of the continued interest in the wealth of spiritual teaching found in the heart-to-heart talks of Kathryn Kuhlman, we have compiled this set of eleven messages.

May you be blessed as you read the contents of this book, and may you be challenged to believe God for yet greater miracles and a more intimate relationship with Jesus Christ through the person of the Holy Spirit.

The Kathryn Kuhlman Foundation

CHAPTER ONE

The Beginning
of Miracles

YE SHALL RECEIVE POWER, AFTER THAT THE HOLY GHOST
IS COME UPON YOU: AND YE SHALL BE WITNESSES UNTO ME
BOTH IN JERUSALEM, AND IN ALL JUDAEA, AND IN SAMARIA,
AND UNTO THE UTTERMOST PART OF THE EARTH.
ACTS 1:8

One of the very first questions that almost every reporter asks me is, "Kathryn Kuhlman, just how did these miracles begin happening in your ministry?" I try to answer the question the best I know how, even as I shall try to answer it for you.

I began preaching when I was very young, and since you can never give to another any more than you have experienced yourself, my messages as I stood behind the pulpit were limited to salvation—how to be born again. Not once did I doubt that wonderful spiritual transaction that took place in a little Methodist church in Concordia, Missouri, when I was fourteen years old. It was real. It was wonderful. It was my first contact with the Holy Spirit. At that time, however, I was not aware that there was such a person, for I had never seen any outward manifestation of the power of the Holy Spirit.

That Sunday morning in the Methodist Church, which probably did not hold any more than one hundred people, something happened to Joe Kuhlman's girl. Sitting next to Mama, sharing the same Methodist hymnal and singing the closing hymn, I began to tremble. I began to shake so hard that I could no longer hold the hymnal in my hand. Little did I know that it was the mighty power of the Holy Spirit—the same power that I have experienced scores of times since but in a greater measure. This was my first contact with the Third Person of the Trinity, and in that moment I knew I needed Jesus to forgive my sins.

Since I had never seen anyone receive Christ as their Savior, I did not know what to do, but many times I had seen new members go forward as they were received into the church. So following their example, I left the place where I was seated, walked to the front of the church and sat down in the first empty seat. It wasn't a struggle. It wasn't even praying. It was a personal experience in which the blood of Jesus Christ, God's Son, cleansed me from all sin. It was glorious! It was real, very real, and I have never doubted it from that moment to this hour. I knew I had been forgiven!

Even as I tell it now, I remember how I wept. The preacher did not know what to do with me. No altar call had been given. In fact, I doubt that an altar call had been given for years in that little church. But I knew something had happened to me, something real and definite, something that nothing could stop. As I sat weeping, Martha Johannssen, a precious lady of the church, slipped over to my side and offered me her handkerchief. She said in a whisper, "Oh, Kathryn, don't cry. You've always been such a good girl." But even as she spoke those words, we both knew that what she said was not quite the truth for I was the most mischievous kid in town.

Walking home that Sunday, I thought the whole world had changed. I thought that Mr. Kroenoke had gotten a new paint job on his house, but the house had not changed—it did not have a fresh coat of paint, it was still the same house. Nothing in Concordia had changed—except me. I was the one who had changed.

Now Papa never overworked this thing of going to church, which is putting it mildly. Sure, at Christmas when I gave a recitation—or on *very special* occasions— he was there. So that Sunday when I returned home, Papa was standing in the kitchen. I rushed over to him and said: "Papa, something has happened to me! Jesus has come into my heart!" Whether or not he understood I'm not quite sure. I never knew. He just looked at me, happy because I was so happy, and said, "I'm glad."

It was the beginning of something that changed my whole life. All I knew was the glorious new birth experience, and when I went to preach to those farmers in Idaho, I could tell them nothing more than what I had experienced—that Jesus would forgive their sins. And do you know that I am still getting letters from some of those precious farmers and members of their families? Many write and say things like: "We remember you well. We remember you as a young girl who came to our church, one who preached so simply. We see you on television now and you haven't changed." That is the greatest compliment they can pay me, to say that I have not changed. But why should I change? The gospel is the same. The Word of God is the same, and I pray I will never change.

In those early years I would wait until the farmers were finished with their milking, their plowing, their harvesting, before I held my meetings. When it was dark they would file in one by one for the services. I have preached in almost every little crossroad town in Idaho: Emmett, Filer, Caldwell. Nobody really wanted me, and I did not blame them much, but I offered my services anyway. Where the churches were closed, where they had no preacher, there is where I went and I would say, "Your church is closed and you have nothing to lose and you might gain something if you allow me to preach."

That was the start of my spiritual education. Today it seems that so many young folks want to begin at the top rung of the ladder—with instant fame or as a celebrity. I know where I began, from whence I have come, and I shall never forget it.

I remember once when I was in my kitchen at five o'clock one Sunday morning preparing my sermon to deliver in Youngstown, Ohio. The people of this ministry are very special. They are extremely faithful, standing behind me through thick and thin, and I always try to give them the best that I have. It had been late Saturday night when I returned to Pittsburgh by plane. I had had a busy week filled with calls from all over the world—an invitation to Australia, three from England, a call from a prominent pastor urging me to come to Sweden, and one to minister in Norway.

In that early morning hour, weary in body, for I had had only a little rest, I found myself weeping, my tears falling on my open Bible. Alone in the house I looked up and spoke audibly to my Heavenly Father, just as though I could see Him. I asked: "Why didn't You allow all of this to happen to me when I was sixteen or seventeen years old? I never got tired in body then. Why did You wait so long?"

It was true. I didn't know what weariness really was when I was young. I could ride those buses all night on my way to the next little farm town and then preach all the next day. I never needed sleep. Oh, often I was hungry and sometimes all I had was the price of a bowl of soup and a bread roll—they were five cents then—but I was never tired in body, and I was doing exactly what I wanted to do and loving every minute of it.

It was not an audible voice that spoke in answer to my question. I would tell you an untruth if I said that I heard God's voice, but He did answer me as definitely as if I could see Him and hear His voice. This is what He said: "Kathryn, had I given it to you then, you would have blown the whole thing."

I was stunned for a moment, but I knew exactly what God meant. Exactly! There had to be a growing process first, a time of learning, a time of schooling. But He did not choose to send me to some seminary, nor to a university. I was given the greatest Teacher in the whole world—the Holy Spirit. And when He is your teacher you get your theology straight. Oh, how I studied my Bible. I was so hungry for the Word of God.

Now in those early days, I never thought of staying at a hotel. In fact, in the rural sections where I preached they had no hotels or motels either. Sometimes a deacon of the church would let me stay in his guest room, where it was often cold in the winter. Most homes in those days had no central heating, so naturally there was little warmth in their guest rooms. To make matters worse, it seemed that in every one of those spare rooms, enormous heavy-framed portraits of someone's grandpa and grandma hung on the walls, and they all looked so grim and stern. I slept under layers of blankets to keep from freezing, and then when I opened my eyes in the morning, the unsmiling, icy stares of someone's ancestors frowned down at me.

How many times I would lie on my stomach on the bed, fully dressed but huddled under the quilts to keep warm, poring over the Word of God, studying it, reading it. I know who was my teacher. I know why I know what I know today regarding the Word of God. It did not just happen. One never gets something for nothing, even when it comes to spiritual things. Someone once said of me, "Kathryn Kuhlman is a lucky person." But it was not luck. I know the price I paid.

I preached salvation throughout Idaho to everyone who would listen. Gradually, however, I began to realize there was someone besides the Father and the Son—there was this Third Person of the Trinity. I felt compelled to know more regarding Him, and as I began searching and studying God's Word, I could see that divine healing also was in the atonement. You cannot study the Word of God with an open heart and an open mind without realizing that healing for the physical body, healing for the whole person, is in the Bible.

When Jesus died on the Cross, when He cried, "It is finished," He not only died for our sins, He died for the whole person. In Isaiah 53:5 we read, "He was wounded for our transgressions, he was bruised for our iniquities … and with his stripes we are healed." We partake of the bread and the wine at the communion table and everyone knows what the wine represents—the shed blood of Jesus Christ. At the first Passover, the lamb without blemish was killed, and the blood was sprinkled on the door posts of the house. That blood represented the One who was to come in the future, the Lamb of God. "It is the blood that maketh an atonement for the soul" (Leviticus 17:11). Perfect blood was shed for our sins—the blood of the Son of the living God.

But, at that first Passover, there was something *more* than the blood. They were told to eat of the flesh of the lamb. What did the flesh represent? What does the bread represent when we take communion? It is His body broken on the Cross: "With his stripes we are healed." There is healing for you and for me through the broken body of the Son of the living God. Every time you take communion, the wine is for the soul, representing the blood of Jesus Christ that makes an atonement for the soul. The bread has nothing to do with our forgiveness of sins, it is for the healing of our bodies. There is healing for the *whole person* through Jesus Christ the Son of God. In every church where communion is served, and they partake of that bread, there should also be the healing for the body.

I saw it! The Holy Spirit had revealed this truth to my heart. "Flesh and blood hath not revealed this unto thee, but my Father which is in heaven" (Matthew 16:17). These things are only spiritually revealed, and that is why sometimes the most uneducated person knows more about the deep truths of God's Word than someone who has spent years attaining knowledge through much education.

I saw God's provision for healing in the Bible, but I could not see scriptural healing taking place as I watched many evangelists who had long healing lines. Whether or not I ever saw a miracle, however, I knew that provision was made for the healing of the physical according to the Word of God. No one being healed did not alter God's Word one iota. If I lived and died and never saw a miracle of healing of the physical, it would not change God's Word. God said it. He made provision for it. It was there in His Word and I wanted it. I had to experience it for myself.

I began to seek earnestly for the answer, attending many services, and one in particular stands out in my memory. I went there seeking but I did not find what I sought. I began to weep and left the meeting still weeping, having no control of my tears. All that I could seem to say were the same words that Mary Magdalene uttered when she found the tomb empty on that first Easter morning: "They have taken away my Lord and I know not where they have laid him" (John 20:2).

All that night I wept uncontrollably. I cried all the next day. I could not stop. I was so hungry and so thirsty for the answers to my questions, and I knew God promised, "Blessed are they which do hunger and thirst after righteousness: for they shall be filled" (Matthew 5:6). I was confident therefore that God would not mock that hunger in my heart, so I did not give up seeking. I knew the answer was there for me. I was determined to wait on God.

And then it happened! It was in Franklin, Pennsylvania, in the old Billy Sunday Tabernacle. Think what a place God chose. I was standing on the same platform where Billy Sunday had stood preaching the gospel years and years previous to that night. I had gone to Franklin by faith, not knowing what I would find there. In the first service there were only thirty-eight people. In the next service there were nearly two hundred people. After that the tabernacle never held the crowds.

It was in that third service, as I was preaching on the Holy Spirit, sharing with the people the little that I knew about that Third Person of the Trinity, that a woman stood up and asked, "Kathryn, may I say something?"

I answered, "Of course you may."

She stated very simply, "Last night while you were preaching, I was healed."

I was shocked. I asked, "How do you know?"

She replied: "Because I had a tumor that had been diagnosed by my doctor. While you were preaching, something happened in my body and I was so sure that

9

I was healed that I went back to my doctor and had it verified today. He could not find a tumor!"

That was the first healing that took place in this ministry. It happened without the laying on of hands, without any special prayer. It just happened as a woman sat in the audience in Franklin, Pennsylvania, while I was preaching on the power of the Holy Spirit. Since that time there have been thousands and thousands of healings. What is the secret? It is the Third Person of the Trinity!

The services continued in Franklin and the next great miracle took place the following Sunday. That was when I realized something was happening, that I had tapped some great spiritual resource. I was not sure just how it happened, but I knew the Holy Spirit had something to do with it. Oh, the thrill, the joy, the expectancy that was mine! But there was so little that I knew and understood about this Person of the Trinity.

I preached again on His mighty power that next Sunday. George Orr, a Methodist from Grove City, Pennsylvania, was in the service with his wife. He was receiving compensation for the loss of his right eye injured in an accident in the foundry where he worked. All the papers were on file to verify his disability. There was no mistake about it. He had suffered greatly, and to make matters worse, the sight of his left eye was rapidly deteriorating.

Riding home from that Sunday service with his wife and friends, George suddenly realized he could see markings along the road. As they crested a hill, he turned to his wife and asked, "Did something just now happen to the sunlight?" She looked at him without answering, and he went on to explain that it appeared that the sun suddenly burst forth from behind a cloud.

His wife said, "No, I didn't notice anything strange."

Little more was said as they continued on their way home. When George walked into the kitchen, the first thing he saw was the clock. Standing there in the doorway he realized he could see the clock clearly—that both eyes were perfect! Sight had been restored to the eye for which he was receiving total compensation, and his deteriorating eye was now normal.

No one had laid hands on George Orr. No one had prayed for him. I was not there. But something glorious had happened! Mr. Orr came back to the service the next night and told what had happened. His face was shining, and he did not need anyone to tell him that physical healing was real—*he could see!*

The secret to that miracle? What was it? There was nowhere to go for the answer but to God's Word, and as I sought, my understanding was quickened. I could picture the three persons of the Trinity seated at a great conference table planning mankind's salvation. Perfect, sinless blood alone could atone for man's sins, and only the Son of God could measure up, for He was absolute deity, absolute divinity, the very Son of the living God. But to pay the price for man's salvation would mean that He must come in the form of flesh, and so He offered Himself to the Father through the Holy Spirit.

Sometimes I think of those who try to minimize the power of the Holy Spirit, refusing to accept His person and power. Remember, if Jesus could trust Him, if Jesus staked everything that He had on the Holy Spirit, surely you and I can afford to trust the Holy Spirit. Jesus knew the Holy Spirit. He knew the mighty Third Person of the Trinity to a greater degree than any human being has ever known Him. Even with all the spiritual insight that the apostle Paul possessed, with all the secrets God entrusted to him, with all the glory he experienced, Paul never knew the power and the person of the Holy Spirit as Jesus knew Him. Nobody ever has. The Holy Spirit was the resurrection power and Jesus knew it. He was the power of the Trinity. Jesus knew it. Jesus had faith and full confidence in the Holy Spirit, and I believe that Jesus, knowing all that was involved as He offered Himself as a sacrifice for mankind's sins, turned first of all to the Holy Spirit and said: "If You will be with Me, if You will come too, I will go."

I believe the Holy Spirit understood perfectly and nodded His head in agreement. Then it was that God gave His only begotten Son so that you and I might have eternal life. Jesus came in the form of flesh, came as a babe in a manger—literally God in the flesh. He grew to manhood, but the three Persons of the Trinity were not united again until that hour when Jesus came up out of the waters of baptism. What a glorious moment when Jesus came up out of those waters and the voice of God said: "This is my beloved Son, in whom I am well pleased" (Matthew 3:17). No man or woman can ever stand before the Creator or before the judgment seat of God and say, "I didn't know who Jesus was." God

Himself left no doubt in the mind of any human being. No one can plead ignorance, for God Himself spoke to those gathered at the Jordan River that day and to all generations to come, when He said: "This is my beloved Son, in whom I am well pleased."

In that moment something happened. The Holy Spirit came upon Jesus in the likeness of a dove. It must have been one of the greatest and most glorious thrills that the Master experienced when He walked in the flesh upon this earth. I can almost hear the Holy Spirit whispering to Him: "I'm here now and things will happen. We are running on schedule. I am keeping my part of the agreement. You keep Yours, and mankind will have salvation for the whole man. I am here!"

Then it was that miracles could begin happening. I know, like others I talk about the miracles that *Jesus* did. We read about the miracles in the ministry of Jesus, and we always think of *Jesus* performing those miracles. But, in reality, the miracles were the result of the power of the *Holy Spirit*.

When Jesus walked this old earth He was as much God as though He were not man, and He was as much man as though He were not God. So when He was tempted of the devil He could have yielded to those temptations. That confrontation in the wilderness was not the first time that Jesus and Satan had met. They knew each other well. Jesus knew Satan before he became Satan, even when he was called Lucifer and was one of the chief angels given great power by God his Creator. Jesus knew Lucifer before his fall. He knew him before he said in his heart, "I will be like the most High" (Isaiah

14:14) and rebelled against God. When God thrust him out of heaven, Lucifer, who had walked in the midst of the stones of fire (Ezekiel 28:14), became the opposite of all he had been. We know him today as Satan, the prince of darkness, the accuser, the adversary, the devil.

No, that was not the first time that Jesus and the devil met face to face. When the devil stood before Jesus and offered Him the title deed to this planet earth if He would bow down and serve him, Jesus knew that he was not lying. This very hour, Satan still holds the title deed to this earth where he once ruled over thousands and thousands, perhaps even millions of angels. This earth was his great empire, for when God created Lucifer He gave him the title deed to this earth and he still holds it.

Jesus could have turned to him and said, "You are a liar," but Jesus knew that Satan was not lying, and not until Jesus returns to earth as King of kings and Lord of lords will Satan forfeit the title deed to this planet earth. That is one reason why Satan is working overtime. He knows that his days and hours are numbered. His time is short as a great world ruler. There is coming a day when the surface of this earth will be renovated by fire and the city of New Jerusalem as seen by the apostle John will come down (Revelation 21:2), and this old planet will become our eternal home. In that day Jesus Himself will hold the title deed to this planet, and we will have a part in that great inheritance and will rule and reign with Him.

Those miracles during the ministry of Jesus were performed by the Holy Spirit. Jesus had come to earth in the form of flesh, and He knew it was the power of the Holy Spirit that was responsible for those miracles, that He was dependent on the Holy Spirit, the Third Person of the Trinity, for every miracle that took place in His ministry. So before Jesus went back to glory to take His position of High Priest at the right hand of God the Father, He made provision to give a gift to His Church, of which He is the head. The greatest gift that He could bequeath was the One who had been so faithful and true to Him while He walked this earth in the form of flesh, the One who had never left or disappointed Him, the One who was the power of the Godhead. This gift, the Holy Spirit, was promised in His last words before His ascension to the Father: "Ye shall receive power, after that the Holy Ghost is come upon you" (Acts 1:8).

You see, giving is a natural product of love and love is something you do. The living Church—this body of believers—was the Father's gift to Jesus the Son, and Jesus prayed for "these that thou hast given me" in His prayer of intercession to the Father before He went to the Cross (John 17:11). Following the Father's example of love, Jesus wanted to give a gift to His Church, to those whom God has given to Him—and He gave the Holy Spirit.

I wish I could stand on the highest mountain top and shout it until every man, every woman, every priest, every rabbi, every minister who is behind the pulpit could know and hear and understand. This wonderful gift that Jesus has given to His body of believers is a sacred and a holy gift. What greater gift could Jesus give than the One who had been responsible for the miracles performed through His ministry, the One who had empowered

Him, whose power had raised Him from the grave—the Holy Spirit?

Jesus remembered the great manifestations of the power of the Third Person of the Trinity. He knew what a great comforter the Holy Spirit had been to Him (the Hebrew word *parakletos*, translated *comforter* in the KJV, can also be rendered *intercessor, advocate, counselor, helper, standby,* or *strengthener*). He knew the Holy Spirit had been His strengthener during those days of loneliness when He was spat upon and ridiculed, and when it seemed the whole world did not understand Him. All men, even His disciples for a time, forsook Him. But the Holy Spirit was always with Him, strengthening Him. The Holy Spirit was the mighty resurrection power on that first Easter morning, giving Jesus victory over death and the grave.

Do you know the glorious strengthening power of the Holy Spirit? Paul did. Perhaps he felt as I do at this moment as I think about the spiritual experiences, the closeness and the deepness and the glory of those spiritual encounters I have known. Jesus is so merciful, and God's love cannot be fathomed. Where would any of us be without the mercy of the Lord or without the love of God? But do not stop there. We have the fellowship of the Holy Spirit, that closeness, that oneness in the midnight hour when it is so dark. Jesus was not defeated in the hour of temptation because of the power and the presence of the Holy Spirit.

Neither can you or I be victorious in our own strength. We cannot be strong except in the power of the Holy Spirit. Do you know Him in that sense? Jesus knew Him. Jesus understood. Jesus knew the secret of His earthly victory and that was the reason He promised, "Ye shall receive power." What power? The same power that had been manifested in His ministry and in His daily life. Do you see it? If only I had the ability to put what I know into words. It was the greatest day of my life when I learned about the Holy Spirit, it changed my ministry.

If you're a minister, are you lacking results in your ministry? Are you discouraged? Do you dread going into your pulpit, dread facing your congregation Sunday after Sunday? Sometimes you wish you could be an ordinary somebody instead of a minister. It is so discouraging when you see no results. If you are not satisfied, I urge you to turn everything, your whole ministry, over to the Holy Spirit. Turn yourself and your will over to the Holy Spirit. If you do, you will have a new ministry. You will be a new person, you will have a new congregation. There will be a new vision there and you will get results.

"Ye shall receive power, after that the Holy Ghost is come upon you." What happened on the day of Pentecost? The Holy Spirit came. Jesus promised He would come and we know that Jesus arrived in heaven safely and on schedule because the Holy Spirit arrived on schedule. Jesus said, "It is expedient for you that I go away: for if I go not away, the Comforter will not come unto you; but if I depart, I will send him unto you" (John 16:7).

In other words, Jesus was saying that He had to go back to take the position of great High Priest at the right hand of God the Father; and after His arrival in glory,

He would send the Holy Spirit. We would know that He arrived safely, that He had assumed His position of High Priest, that everything was working on schedule, when the Holy Spirit came as He said He would come.

Jesus kept His promise. The one hundred and twenty were filled with the Holy Spirit on the first Day of Pentecost. Things happened! These were exciting times in the early church. But remember something: we talk about the Day of Pentecost as if it were in the past. *We are still living in the Day of Pentecost!*

Today is the Day of Pentecost, and we have every right to have the same things happening in our churches this hour as happened on the first Day of Pentecost. Why? Because it is the person of the Holy Spirit who is the power. The Day of Pentecost will *not* come to an end until the Holy Spirit leaves, and when the Holy Spirit goes, He will take the Church, the members of the Body of Christ, with Him. We call it the *Rapture of the Church*, or the *Great Catching Up*, and only then will come the close of this dispensation, the end of the Day of Pentecost.

What is the secret to the power in this ministry? The secret is found in the Person of the Holy Spirit. I have chosen to accept the gift that Jesus left for me, and you will never regret it if you accept His gift, too.

Chapter Two

The Will of God

Life is the most important thing in the whole world. Next to the soul, there is nothing—absolutely nothing—on this Earth that is more important to God than human life. We have come to the day and hour, however, when life seems mighty cheap. Pro's and con's concerning the issue of abortion are openly discussed. Our daily newspapers are filled with accounts of one disaster after another, and every day newscasters report tragedies involving highway or plane accidents that claimed lives, often hundreds of lives. We sympathize but we fold the paper and put it aside. We turn off the radio or television set, dismissing it all so easily. Life has become cheap according to humanity's sense of value.

Yet, in the sight of God, there is nothing more priceless, there is no greater treasure, and no earthly property has greater value than human life. Life is so priceless that He gave a commandment that no man has the authority to take another's life. In the hands of God alone there rests the complete power to give life, and the sovereign authority to take human life. To protect all human life, God said, "Thou shalt not kill" (Exodus 20:13).

19

Human beings are so important in God's sight that He has a blueprint in heaven for each person, detailing a plan for every life. We read in the Lord's Prayer: "Thy will be done in earth as it is in heaven" (Matthew 6:10), and we see at a glance by this Scripture that there is a definite will in heaven for each life. Thus there is also a will for every human being here on earth. The will as recorded in heaven is God's will. The will that is exercised on earth is our will. They are two wills, separate and apart from each other.

Every time I hold a precious baby in my arms dedicating it to God, I pray what I consider the greatest prayer that I can pray for that tiny bit of flesh—that its life will be lived according to God's perfect will. I can pray no greater prayer, for I am convinced beyond a shadow of a doubt that when a little baby gives its first cry and takes its first breath, in the mind of God and in His hand is a perfect blueprint charting the perfect course for that life. God does absolutely nothing indiscriminately. He is perfect precision.

When God spoke the worlds into existence, He had a perfect plan. Long before Jesus came as a babe heralded by the angelic hosts, I believe that the Father, the Son, and the Holy Spirit sat down together at a great conference table and talked over the plan for the redemption of man. There was a precise plan, a perfect blueprint, before Jesus ever offered Himself through the Holy Spirit to be given by God the Father as the atonement for the souls of men. I believe that God had a perfect plan for Abraham, a perfect plan for Elijah and for Moses. He is never careless in His dealings. As you study the Scriptures, you will see a perfect blueprint for the children of Israel, and they

20

are living according to that blueprint as prophesied in God's Word.

God had a perfect plan for the apostle Paul's life, and because He is no respecter of persons, He has a perfect plan for your life and mine—and all the devils in existence could never argue me out of that conviction. I believe it so sincerely that I am deeply affected by a certain portion of the Word of God every time I read it. It has reference to Jesus when He stood before Pilate. These are the words He spoke: "To this end was I born, and for this cause came I into the world" (John 18:37).

Sometimes I may not understand God's dealings in my life, but I know that God has a perfect plan and purpose for me. I did not choose the country in which I was born. I had no control of the century in which I would live. I had no choice of sex, for had I been given a choice I would have chosen to be a man. It would have been a thousand times easier to stand behind the pulpit and preach the gospel had I been born a man. As a woman I had two strikes against me before I started. My work would not have been nearly so hard, because there is so much prejudice against a woman preacher. But I was not given my choice of sex.

Neither did I have a choice when it came to my physical appearance. If I had, God knows I never would have chosen red hair. I had nothing to say about when I came into this world, and I have no control over when I am to leave. All of that is in the hands of an all-wise God.

This very hour there is a precious soul, perhaps a saint of God who is well advanced in years, whose loved ones are on the other shore. She feels so lonely, she is so homesick. She would give anything in the world if Jesus would call her home. She knows of no reason why she should continue to live. Yet she has nothing to say about her going home, and she simply must wait until the Lord says, "It is your time now, come home."

Now I am sure there is someone you have known with seemingly every reason in the world to live, still in the springtime of youth, who was taken "before their time." I cannot tell you why. I only know that there is One at the helm, God Almighty, in whose sight the most precious thing in the whole universe is a human life. We are in His hand, and it lies in His power to give or take human life. He controls the when and the how of death.

You may feel that you are only one of millions of people, and that God has no regard whatsoever for you as an individual. You may feel that I am talking about something that is far out someplace when I tell you that God has a perfect blueprint for your life. But I am not. Did you ever stop to realize that you are so individual to God that no one who has ever been born, no one who will ever be born, no one who is living this hour has the same fingerprints as yours? You will have to admit that this fact makes you mighty personal in the sight of God. Every hour and day of your life is important. You pass this way through life but once, and after this day has passed and the clock strikes the midnight hour, you cannot bring back a single opportunity nor relive a moment of this day. It is gone forever—it is history.

You are a strange combination of the eternal and the material. When you were born and you took that first breath, there entered into that body of yours a soul with eternity for a lifetime. Death cannot touch that soul. The old body will go back to the dust of the earth from whence it came, but there is a part of you, your soul, that is eternal. Nothing can destroy it.

But you were also born with a will, a will separate and apart from the will of anyone else. You are free to exercise that will of yours. You are a free moral agent. You can do with your life whatever you please. There are many people walking the streets of failure, living in defeat, licked by the problems of life, who might have been spiritual giants, leaders, ones who might have lived in victory had they surrendered their wills to the perfect will of God.

That is the reason that no man or woman can ever say that God condemned or sent them to hell. No one can ever place the blame at God's feet for their going to hell. Each of us exercises our own will, choosing whether or not we will receive Christ and the pardon He gave, receive the deity and divinity of God's Son, or reject the whole plan of salvation. We are free moral agents.

Even Jesus Christ Himself, the very Son of the Living God, had a will separate and apart from the will of His Father. Before He paid the price in full through the atonement, the last thing He did was surrender His will to the will of His Father: "Thy will be done in earth, as it is in heaven." The greatest example of full surrender to God's will was given by the Son of God Himself. Even though Jesus had offered Himself through the Holy Spirit to be given for the salvation of the souls of lost mankind, the whole plan could still have been foiled and voided. Jesus had the right to exercise His own will and could have looked up and said, "Father, I cannot go through with it." But instead, in that last moment, He surrendered His will and said, "Nevertheless not my will, but thine be done" (Luke 22:42).

In exactly the same way you have a will that you must exercise. You are responsible for your will. I am responsible for my will, and to explain what I am trying to say let me share with you something that happened when I was not more than fifteen years old.

I was inexperienced, with no learning, yet I knew that I had been born again and that I had been called into the ministry. A dear old saint of God, Brother McCloud, a spiritual giant when in his prime, gave me advice that I shall never forget. Although, looking back now, I realize I didn't have the faintest idea of what he was saying to me. He was lean and lanky, almost emaciated looking, perhaps in his early eighties. I can almost feel those bony hands tightly holding mine as he pressed them together with all the strength he had and looked me directly in the face and said: "Girl, my ministry has come to an end. I have had my day. I will soon be going home but you are young. You have your whole life before you. God has a great work for you to do. There is just one bit of advice I want to give you. It is simply this: *Never get out of the will of God.*"

Smiling, I thanked him but I had no idea, not the slightest idea what he was saying. I was a 15-year-old girl, inexperienced, absolutely ignorant of the rich gems of knowledge that fell from this saint's lips. But I know now. I know today what I did not know then.

I do not fear the power of the devil for I am serving One who has greater power than satanic power. I am not afraid of all the forces of Satan for I belong to One whose power is greater than all his demonic hordes. I am afraid of just one thing—getting out of the will of God. More than anything else in the whole world I covet His perfect will, for when I am in the center of His will, I have His favor, I have His blessing, I have His smile, I have heaven's best. All the power and all the glory of heaven are with me. I am surrounded by His love. All that is His is mine. He will protect me, He will guide me, He will lead me, He will give me His wisdom.

Beloved, the most coveted place in the whole universe is the center of God's perfect will. Yet there are times when the hardest thing is to know God's will, for there is a perfect will and a permissive will of God, and I can prove it from His Word.

Psalm 106:11-15 reads: "And the waters covered their enemies: there was not one of them left. Then believed they his words; they sang his praise." They were on the mountain top, for God had given them victory. But watch! True to human nature: "they soon forgot his works; they waited not for his counsel: but lusted exceedingly in the wilderness, and tempted God in the desert. And he gave them their request; but sent leanness into their soul."

Here we have a concrete example of God giving a people that which they desired, that which they wanted, that which they requested. But it was not His perfect will for them. It was not heaven's best for them, but He gave it to them because they wanted it, they desired it, they sought it. In giving them that which they desired, however, He was giving them His permissive will.

This, beloved, means more to me than I can tell because I have come a long way since I first began in the ministry. I have had to learn the hard way. In fact, it seems to me that I have had to learn everything in my life the hard way. I have been knocked down so often, and I have brought so much trouble on myself. I cannot blame God for a thing I have suffered in my life because, looking back, I see that I brought it all on myself.

I am one of those creatures who is just naturally impetuous. I lack patience. It is part of my natural construction. As I told you before in this message, I was not given the choice where to be born or my sex. Neither did I choose my temperament. I think it would be wonderful to be patient. But what did I get? A nature that is anything but patient. I am so impetuous. Everything has to be done right now. I cannot wait!

Therefore I have found that many times I have received God's permissive will because I could not wait. I walked where angels feared to tread. I prayed, I stormed heaven, I entreated: "Heavenly Father—now—it has to be right now!" He saw the sincerity of my heart and He would not disappoint my confidence in Him. So He said, "All right, child. I will give you that which you have asked. I will answer your prayer, but in answering your prayer, I can only give you heaven's second best." Had I waited a little longer, it would have been much better for me. What did God give me? He gave the desire of my heart, but sent leanness to my soul even as He did to the children of Israel. It was not His best for me. It was not according to His blueprint for my life.

This thing of knowing God's perfect will is one of the hardest things in the world. No one else can tell you what God's perfect will is for your life. People have asked me, "Miss Kuhlman, what is God's perfect will for me?" I could not give them the answer. I have a hard enough time trying to find out God's perfect will for me. No one else can tell another what God's perfect will is for them, just as no one can tell me what God's will is for my life. You, like me, have a hard enough time taking care of God's perfect will for yourself.

But, I will tell you a secret that I learned through years of experience, through many bitter tears and many heartaches. Do you want the will of God for your life? Are you sincere in seeking His will regarding a certain problem? Do you really, conscientiously, want God's will in a given matter? *You will only know His will when you surrender your own will to Him, when you no longer have a will of your own, praying even as Jesus prayed, "Nevertheless not my will but thy will be done."*

Jesus surrendered His will to the will of the Father in the Garden of Gethsemane, and when you can get to the place of full surrender, where you have no will of your own, then you will know God's perfect will, not His permissive will.

That is exactly what Paul meant in Romans 8:26-27: "Likewise the Spirit also helpeth our infirmities: for we know not what we should pray for as we ought." How often we come to that place where we do not know how we should pray. But, Paul continues: "The Spirit itself maketh intercession for us with groanings which cannot be uttered. And he that searcheth the hearts knoweth what is the mind of the Spirit, because he maketh intercession for the saints according to the will of God."

Here Paul is giving us the answer because he, too, had come to the place where he did not know the perfect will of God, when he could not perceive how to pray. Fortunately for us, He gives us the way that he found successful. In other words, this is what Paul did:

I go alone where I can close the door. I surrender my will completely to the will of the Father. I bring myself to the place where I have no will of my own, and then the two wills become as one. I surrender myself to the will of the Father, not knowing how to pray or what His will is. I am quiet and I permit the Holy Spirit, who knows the perfect will of God, to pray through me, in me, and He shows me God's perfect will.

I know now what dear brother McCloud meant. In the perfect will of God, though the waters are sometimes deep, there is a peace of mind, a peace of soul that passes all understanding. In spite of hardships, you can smile even though you do not understand. You can smile as you stand at the open grave. You can smile when the sun has ceased to shine. You can smile when the stones are bruising your feet. You can smile when disappointments come—because you know you are in the center of God's perfect will.

Have you taken that first step into the perfect will of God by receiving Christ into your heart? If you are not a Christian this hour, you are out of the perfect will of God. It is His will, His perfect will that every person should know His Son as Savior and Redeemer. He is not willing that *any* should perish. If you are living outside of this wonderful inheritance, without knowing this relationship of Father and child, it is because you have made the choice. God's first choice for you is a relationship with Him through Jesus Christ, a life of victory.

But God forces no person to live this life in His perfect will. You have been given the choice as a free moral agent to exercise your own will separate and apart from the will of the Holy God. Thousands are doing exactly that today. They are exercising their wills separate and apart from the will of God, and they are living contrary to His will, because they are using their will to live their life as they prefer to live it.

I want you to realize something. If you are exercising your will contrary to the will of God, then you are not receiving His best and you are not receiving what God has for you, heaven's best according to His blueprint in glory.

We were made for God, made in His image and after His likeness, and our hearts are restless until they repose in Him. Our lives are without meaning until we are led by the Holy Spirit in the perfect will of God.

CHAPTER THREE

Victory Over Temptation

Every human being faces temptation. There is never a day, an hour, or a moment that we, as free moral agents, are not confronted with temptations in some form. When Jesus walked this earth, He was as much man in the flesh as though He were not God, and He is well acquainted with the temptations that come to every human being. He is no stranger to the difficulties that can and do beset the soul. Jesus was tempted in the wilderness by the same devil who tempts you and me, but He was as perfect after the temptations as when He entered the wilderness experience—as perfect as if He had never been tempted.

New-born children of God, in the early stages of spiritual development, often do not experience the difficulties and temptations that come after the preliminary interval of spiritual enlightenment is passed. In a sense, God places hedges about new-born Christians, and only as they mature and advance in spiritual things do all the subtle perils harass and plague them on their pathways.

This is where many spiritual leaders have failed. In our eagerness to have men and women receive Christ as Savior, we paint such a rosy picture of the Christian life that the unregenerate feel that there will be no more battles after they receive Christ. They have the misconception that they will no longer have temptations after they are born again, that all of their conflicts will cease following that wonderful spiritual rebirth.

We need to warn young converts that even though they have embarked on a new life, there will be temptations. We dare not forget that the enemy of our souls is very active, and the greater the life of usefulness for God, the greater will be the temptations. We must be on guard! Believe me when I tell you that we will have temptations as long as we are in the body of flesh and living on this planet Earth, and as long as the enemy of our souls is in the same world. I don't care how deeply spiritual you may be, there will be temptations.

I have talked with some who have said that they are on such a spiritual plateau—that they have soared so high spiritually—that they no longer have temptations. When they tell me this, I just smile to myself, but I think: "You are only kidding yourself. You are the only one who is being deceived." I would not argue with that person concerning his relationship with God, or say he is not God's child, or take issue with that person concerning his marvelous spiritual experiences. I would not try to tell him that he has not gone deep into the things of God. I will agree with him completely, but I will dispute any doctrine that says we can get to such a spiritual level that we are never tempted.

Even the apostle Paul, who was among the greatest saints that ever lived, experienced constant warfare within himself regarding his own temptations. He was consecrated, surrendered, and living for God, or God could not have used Paul and given to him the deep spiritual secrets of His power. Yet Paul was constantly aware of the temptations of the flesh that he battled—temptations such as you and I also face. Why? Because he was still in the body of flesh, and this flesh is corrupt. This flesh is mortal. You and I will have temptations as long as there is breath in our mortal bodies, regardless of our depth of spirituality.

As long as one is in the flesh, and as long as this body is corrupt, we must contend with the flesh. James 1:13-15 says: "Let no man say when he is tempted, I am tempted of God; for God cannot be tempted with evil, neither tempteth he any man; but every man is tempted when he is drawn away of his own lust and enticed. Then when lust hath conceived, it bringeth forth sin; and sin, when it is finished, bringeth forth death."

Do not, however, feel as though you have failed God, or do not feel as though you have slipped spiritually and lost some spiritual ground when you are confronted with diverse temptations. The more you pray, the more time you spend in seeking the Lord, the more sensitive you become to the Holy Spirit and the deeper you grow spiritually. At the same time, however, your trials and temptations become greater.

Temptation in itself is not sin. The greatest saint living today will be tempted because the devil is still very much alive, and because every saint of God is still in a body of flesh and that flesh is corrupt. So we will be tempted. We will still encounter the lusts of the flesh in one way or another, but temptation in itself is no sin. Only when we yield to temptation does it become a sin.

I remember something as vividly as though it happened yesterday. When I began my ministry in the State of Idaho I was very young, but I still hear from some of those precious folk from places like Wendall, Caldwell, and Boise where I preached in little Methodist, Presbyterian, and Baptist churches. I recall my thoughts after I had finished my fifth sermon. I was walking down the road on my way back to the room where I spent the night and I wondered: "What more can I preach about? There isn't anything else in the Bible. I have absolutely exhausted the supply of sermons. For the life of me, I can't think of anything else to preach about."

It makes me smile to remember these thoughts, for since that time the Holy Spirit has revealed many deep truths, and I have still only scratched the surface. Do you know the secret? I have grown. If you are a healthy Christian and there is Jesus' divine life in you, there will be spiritual growth and development.

Today I can take you down a dead-end street in a certain town in a certain state where I surrendered *everything* to Jesus—body, soul, and spirit. As I walked there with tears streaming down my face, for the first time in my life it was none of self and all of Him. When I made that full and complete surrender of everything to

Jesus, the Holy Spirit took the empty vessel—and that's all that He asks. *That day was the dawn of the greatest day of my life.* I had no real ministry until I walked down that little dead-end road and surrendered everything to Him.

But know this: The greater the surrender, the greater the temptations. With that filling of the Holy Spirit comes a responsibility that is tremendous, and as we continue to advance in spiritual stature, new and powerful temptations await us on the path. They are there at every turn of the road. There are temptations to work for self-glory, temptations for personal honors and distinctions, temptations for material gain. There are constant temptations. This wonderful truth that I am sharing with you was there the whole time when I thought I had exhausted the supply of sermons to be preached. Because I was so young spiritually, I did not see the full depth of meaning in God's Word. I had to grow, and as I grew and matured, the Holy Spirit revealed the deep spiritual truths to me. They were bread to my soul. I developed. I grew spiritually in exactly the way a baby grows when it is given the right food. First comes the milk, and then a little more substantial food. Before long the child is eating potatoes and vegetables, and then one day the youngster sits up by the side of dad and says: "Daddy, I want steak like you are eating."

The secret is growth, and the more you pray, the more time you spend in meditation and reading God's Word, the greater efforts you put forth working on your soul, the more sensitive you become to the Spirit. As you become more sensitive and spiritual, the more powerful and effective are your prayers and the better work you do for God. As a result, God will use you in a greater way, and you will advance in spiritual things.

But like everything else in the universe, this works in several ways, and you also become more susceptible to forms of temptation that did not confront you when you were a babe in Christ and first set out on the Christian path. Now I know you agree with me that we always have temptations too difficult for us to handle in our own strength, and we sure don't want stronger ones, so you may be asking: "What is the remedy? Where is the answer?"

Your starting place is to see yourself as God sees you. Look yourself directly in the face. To make it very definite, walk over to the nearest mirror, look yourself in the face, and admit your weakness. That is your beginning. With that admission, with that confession, ninety percent of the battle is already won. *All heaven from here on out is on your side.*

But what about the other ten percent? How do we overcome? Here is the answer: "Ye are of God, and have overcome them [spirits of antichrist]: because greater is he that is in you, than he that is in the world" (1 John 4:4).

In all these things we are not fighting against flesh and blood. We are fighting against something that is greater than flesh and blood. There are only two forces in the world—the forces of sin, or Satan, and the forces of God, or righteousness. When you fight against the forces of sin and unrighteousness, you are not fighting against flesh and blood. When you deal with sin, you

36

are fighting against a power over which there is only one power greater—the power of God.

Therefore, I cannot agree with the person who says that these things can be overcome by will power, for in dealing with men and women I discovered long ago that will power is wonderful only as long as it can hold out. But when will power loses its strength and loses its force, then we go down in defeat, and few men and few women have the will power to overcome the power of Satan and sin. *The secret of victory, therefore, is the greater power of the indwelling Christ.*

Let me make yet a further statement that may surprise you, but it is true: You will never get victory over sin by *fighting* it, because you are fighting a losing battle. Yes, Paul exhorts us to "fight the good fight," but he adds, "of faith" (1 Timothy 6:12). He did not say to fight the good fight to overcome our *sins.* He urges us to "fight the good *fight of faith.*" Now a fight of faith cannot be a struggle.

It is true that James said, "Resist the devil" (James 4:7), but how? With our hands? Through will power? Surely not! Peter said, "Whom resist steadfast in the faith" (1 Peter 5:9). We are to stand, not struggle, having done all things, *stand.* The shield of faith is able to quench all the fiery darts of the evil one (Ephesians 6:16). Faith requires nothing on our part. *Faith lets God do it all.* Jesus Christ has won the victory for you and for me. That is why Paul said, "I live, yet not I but Christ liveth in me" (Galatians 2:20). The secret of victory is the indwelling Christ. Victory is in *trusting*, not *trying.* "Whatsoever is born of God overcometh the world: and this is the victory that overcometh the world, even our faith" (1 John 5:4).

Some have said that a person who tries by strenuous effort to resist or to struggle against sin until it is conquered, is growing in grace. If that is so, then how is it that all growth takes place without effort? Our Lord Himself asked, "Which of you by taking thought can add one cubit unto his stature?" (Matthew 6:27). What is true of our physical growth is true of our spiritual growth as well.

First of all, take physical growth. How is growth secured? By air, food, exercise—all these insure physical growth. We do not think about the growth of our body. If we breathe in good air, if we partake of good substantial food, if we exercise, strong physical growth follows.

And so, if our spiritual life is sustained by the Holy Spirit within and around us—if it is nourished by Jesus Christ, who is the Bread of God—our spiritual life will exercise itself in good works, and there will automatically be growth. There is a wondrous growth *in* grace, but there is no growth *into* grace because sin hinders this growth, and struggling against sin cannot help the growth.

In other words, let's just be very practical about the whole thing. You admit there is sin in your life and the admission itself brings to you ninety percent of the victory. You look up and confess your sin to God and say: "Forgive all the harm that I have done through this sin in my life. I'm sorry." Immediately after the sin is confessed, God forgives you, and you look up and throw yourself completely on His mercy. Daily you say, "Dear Lord, I want You to fill this heart of mine. Give me Your thoughts. Give me Your mind. Indwell this heart of mine so that there will be no room for that sin that has so easily beset me and defeated me in the past."

Jesus came forth from the temptations in the wilderness as the mighty conqueror and victor—completely sinless, the very Son of the living God. He is your representative, and He is mine. Therefore you and I need never be defeated on a single score or in the face of any temptation unless we consent to it. Romans 8:35-39 says:

Who shall separate us from the love of Christ? Shall tribulation, or distress, or persecution, or famine, or nakedness, or peril, or sword?

As it is written, for thy sake we are killed all the day long; we are accounted as sheep for the slaughter.

Nay, in all these things we are more than conquerors through him that loved us.

For I am persuaded, that neither death, nor life, nor angels, nor principalities, nor powers, nor things present, nor things to come.

Nor height, nor depth, nor any other creature shall be able to separate us from the love of God, which is in Christ Jesus our Lord.

We face temptations with the confidence that in Christ Jesus our Lord we *are* victorious.

CHAPTER FOUR

Salvation Is Somebody, Not Something

No one can ever dispute the fact that there is absolutely nothing so hopelessly still or quite so dead as a corpse. Nothing. No doctor, no scientist has yet been able to breathe life into a dead body. Even so, the sinner is just as hopeless without Christ. Without Christ, the sinner is spiritually dead—dead in trespasses and sins. The apostle Paul wrote, "They that are in the flesh cannot please God" (Romans 8:8), and Jesus emphasized this same truth when He said, "It is the spirit that quickeneth; the flesh profiteth nothing: the words that I speak unto you, they are spirit, and they are life" (John 6:63). He also said, "He that heareth my word and believeth on him that sent me, hath everlasting life, and shall not come into condemnation [shall not come under judgment], but is passed from death unto life" (John 5:24).

Salvation is the miracle of receiving life. A miracle happened to you when the Lord Jesus Christ touched your life with His own nail-scarred hand and gave to you

41

new life with His nature. That is exactly what we mean when we talk about being born again. Salvation is not something *you* do, it is something the *Christ* does when you receive Him. He is the one who does it.

To prove this statement I give you this Scripture: "But as many as received him, to them gave he power to become the sons of God, even to them that believe on his name" (John 1:12).

Therefore, salvation is something that Christ does when you receive him. It is not something that *you* do. Of course you must come to Him, demonstrating active faith on your part. You must be willing, but from there on out Christ does the rest. He is the One who gives you eternal life.

Listen to Andrew's words to Simon Peter "We found the Messiah," which is being interpreted, the Christ" (John 1:41). Listen to Philip as he speaks to Nathanael regarding his experience of conversion: "We have found him [a person], of whom Moses in the law and the prophets did write, Jesus of Nazareth, the son of Joseph" (John 1:45). Then hear the words of the woman of Samaria: "Come, see a man, which told me all things that ever I did; is not this the Christ?" (John 4:29). Finally, are there words more thrilling than Paul's when he stood before King Agrippa? I can almost see the glory on is face as he speaks:

At midday, O king, I saw in he way a light from heaven ... I heard a voice speaking unto me ... and I said, Who art thou, Lord? And he said, I am Jesus whom thou persecutest. But rise and stand upon they feet; for I have appeared unto thee for this purpose, to make thee a minister and a witness both of these things which thou hast seen, and of those things in the which I will appear unto thee (Acts 26:13-16).

This very moment, at the heart of your faith is a person. It is a person who gives you eternal life—His life. That is why I say that salvation is not *something* it is *somebody*. When you are saved, when you are born again, you meet a person with a very definite personality. You open your life to Christ, and you embark on a life lived under His control. Paul said: "I know whom [not something, but somebody] I have believed, and am persuaded that he is able to keep that which I have committed unto him [a person] against that day" (2 Timothy 1:12). *Paul's life was not committed to something, but to a definite person—Jesus Christ.*

This is what happened to you when yo invited Christ into your life. You experienced a miracle. You met a person, and you became part of an eternal transaction. Doesn't that do something to you? You see, God could not show us Himself except through another self, one who would be in human surroundings and who would speak the language we speak. Jesus was here in the place of God, speaking the language of the man on the street, manifesting God in understandable terms.

Christ loves you. He understands you. He hears your prayers of confession. As you talk to Him, you are not talking to something but to a person. Life with Christ is the only life to live, for with Him there is assurance. He is there underneath all the uncertainties of human existence, and you can rest in the confidence that—living or dying—you belong to Him and He belongs to you.

43

CHAPTER FIVE

Troubles

Those who have followed this ministry through the years have heard me say these words hundreds of times: *No matter what our troubles are, as long as God is still on His throne and hears and answers prayer, and just so long as your faith in Him is still intact, everything will come out all right!*

Remember something—I do not just say these words, I believe that statement with every atom of my being.

Trouble has a way of stalking down the road and meeting us so many times when we least expect it, and it may befall us without our being personally responsible or even directly the cause of it. Many times trouble is beyond our control, but we should remember that trouble, as well as the hours of sunshine, has a place in shaping our lives and forming our characters.

Trouble and severe testing are not necessarily signs of sin or of failure or a lack of spirituality. In fact, trouble very often is a sign of spirituality—a sign of growth that God must test and prove—for we are God's workmanship. When trouble or sorrow or affliction comes into the life of a Christian, one of the cruelest things that anyone can do is pass judgment and say that it is a result of sin. Nothing could be further from the truth.

Many people have the notion that the life of a Christian is, or should be, something of a charmed life, void of trouble or testing, without tribulation and suffering. Such people hold an absolutely impossible and unscriptural concept and ideal of real Christian living. They do not know Christian experience or the Bible. Here are a few portions of the Word of God in this regard:

1. *Man is born unto trouble, as the sparks fly upward* (Job 5:7).

2. *Many are the afflictions of the righteous; but the Lord delivereth him out of them all* (Psalm 34:19).

3. *For our light affliction, which is but for a moment, worketh for us a far more exceeding and eternal weight of glory* (2 Corinthians 4:17).

4. *In the world ye shall have tribulation; but be of good cheer; I have overcome the world* (John 16:33).

Now don't stop there. There's more. For example, Romans 5:3: "And not only so, but we glory in tribulations also; knowing that tribulation worketh patience." Here is my point. We who are Christians must recognize and be convinced in our hearts that trouble is not designed to defeat us. It is not a mere nuisance or a cruelty. It is one of the corrective elements in living, and we must learn how to use it. Many problems would be solved if only we would take a positive and a constructive attitude and view trouble as one of the agents, or a mighty instrument, that

God has placed in our hands for the shaping of character and the releasing of potential power. Trouble can literally be an angel in disguise.

I urge you to get serious about this now. How do you use trouble? How did you use it a year ago? Six months ago? Yesterday? You cannot reason with trouble. She is utterly unreasonable, but she can be used. The question, however, is *how*?

First of all, put aside the erroneous thought that if you are good and a really spiritual Christian who is totally yielded and consecrated to God you will live a charmed life and God will spare you from trouble and disappointment. No, my friend. To reach a lofty place of consecration and yieldedness is only to make you a fit candidate for tribulation and persecution: "All that will live godly in Christ Jesus shall suffer persecution" (2 Timothy 3:12).

Tribulation is a word that God uses in relation to saints. The word means "threshing." The ancient thresher did not thresh weeds, he threshed golden wheat in order that the grain would separate from the sticks, stubble, and chaff. *The thresher was after grain!*

Our heavenly Father also is after grain. God's Word says, "Tribulation worketh patience (Romans 5:3). In other words, the golden grain of patience and the qualities of long-suffering and kindness come by way of threshing—by way of tribulation and trouble. Do not misunderstand me, however; I am not saying that trouble alone makes us strong and noble, or that is possesses some mystical, transforming power. That is not what I am saying. I am dealing with you as a Christian who believes that "all things work together for good to them that love God, to them who are the called according to his purpose" (Romans 8:28). That text is not for Christians whose lives are not surrendered to Christ, but to Christians who, through the indwelling Holy Spirit, permit troubles to become God's agents that will bring forth the best in them.

Beloved, I caution you to be careful how you act when trouble comes. In itself, trouble is neutral or passive, and the whole matter depends upon how you use it. As part of humanity you will have trouble. I don't care *who* you are. What makes the difference is how you use that trouble—your attitude toward it.

I have noticed a two-fold reaction in the lives of people as they deal with difficulty or tragedy. In some cases it will break them in spirit, melting the hardness and bringing them into a helplessness before God that He uses to generate spiritual growth. Trouble can make anyone a bigger and better person. But it can also throw people upon their own feeble resources and human reasonings. Trouble, however, cannot be reasoned with, and if Christians choose to deal with trouble by drawing solely upon their own frail resources and human reasonings, it will harden their spirits and make them critical and cynical.

That brings up a question: *How can we handle trouble?* First we have to face the trouble and acknowledge that we have to do something about it. We cannot ignore it, sweep it under the rug, and act as though it never happened. It will either make us bitter or it will be a tool to produce growth in character and a deeper spiritual life. We are never quite the same after trouble comes into our lives. *It will make us bitter or better.*

Notice how very similar those two words are: *bitter* and *better.* When we change just one letter—and "e" to an "i"—that alters the whole outcome and result. When the "I" keeps out of the difficulty, life is always better. But when the "I" is allowed to mix in the trouble, we become bitter and hard, critical and cynical. Too many times this "I"—the ego—gets in the way and is hurt, and it then distorts things so that they are not seen as they truly are or should be seen. You and I are not living for only today—this hour or this minute. It takes a quiet heart, peace of spirit, clear vision, and a long range view of life beyond this moment to interpret trouble in terms of strength and growth of character.

Needless to say, I am sure you have dealt with those that I call *little souls*—those who get their feelings hurt almost instantly over the smallest things. Sometimes the ego within is unduly important and consequently easily hurt or flattered. In such cases, they feel they must have everything revolving around them, hence everything relates directly to the self within.

The greatest example we have of a really big soul is Job. The Word of God tells us that Job was "a blameless and upright man, one who fears God and shuns evil" (Job 1:8 NKJV). Rustlers stole is cattle and his horses. His sheep were struck by lightning, his camels were taken by thieves, and all the keepers and shepherds were killed except for a few. His sons and daughters were killed by a great wind. In the face of all this trouble, what did Job do? He rent his garments, shaved his head, and fell on the ground and worshipped God (Job 1:20). Job was a man with passions like yours and mine, which causes me to wonder what I would have done under similar circumstances. But, after all of this happened, we read in verse 22 that, "In all this Job did not sin or charge God with wrong" (NJKV).

Was that all? No! Job's health was next attacked, and his body was covered with ulcer-like boils. Then his wife nagged him and said, "Why do you hold to your faith? Curse God and die" (Job 2:9). Soon after, his friends rebuked and forsook him. Do you wonder what you would have done under those mounting circumstances?

It was dark—very dark—or Job, and perhaps at this very moment, you are groping in like darkness as you read these word. But always remember that as surely as there is the midnight hour, morning will come. It can be so dark at 2 o'clock, at 3 o'clock, at 4 o'clock; but morning will come. Just as morning came for Job, morning will come for you, too.

In the last chapter of the Book of Job, we read that Job was rewarded with twice what he had before. God blessed Job's latter end more than his beginning.

Need I say more? Is not the moral of the story of Job the spiritual principle the Holy Spirit is showing us, obvious? You and I must be careful how we react when troubles come. Be careful how we respond n the face of difficulty and trial. When adversity and misfortune are our lot, that, my friend, is the time to look up and to trust God, for He is in control. *And He never makes a mistake.*

CHAPTER SIX

Your Attitude
Toward Life

Sometimes I feel that this generation knows more about life than any generation of the past, yet they do not know how to live it. Life is vitally important. Your life is as significant as mine, for Jesus' words reveal that He has a plan for everyone. The Scripture states: "To every man his work" (Mark 13:34). It does not say to every man "a work," nor to every man "some work," but to every man his work. So my question is simply this: *Have you found the plan that God has for you?*

It is not a matter of chance or accident or luck that you and I are here on earth. I do not believe that there is such a thing as luck. God made each of us and put us here for a definite purpose. The important question is this: *Have we found what that purpose is?* Have we discovered what niche God would have us fill? He has one for me, and one for you. I know what God would have me do. Have you found the work that He would

51

have you carry out? He has a definite work for you, and that involves the matter of your attitude toward life.

I would therefore like us to look into the attitude of two outstanding men mentioned in the Bible. They are Solomon of the Old Testament, and Paul of the New Testament. Through the years Solomon made disastrous abuse of life, and became one of the most cynical pessimists the world has ever known. Finally, however, before his day was done, he was recovered. But for many years his life was wretched, a misery reflected in his own words: "Then I looked on all the works that my hands had wrought, and on the labor that I had labored to do: and, behold, all was vanity and vexation of spirit, and there was no profit under the sun" (Ecclesiastes 2:11).

How different was the attitude of the apostle Paul, who looked out upon the vast beyond toward which we are all traveling, and said with a triumph that we can feel this very hour as we read his words: "The time of my departure is at hand. I have fought a good fight, I have finished my course, I have kept the faith: henceforth there is laid up for me a crown of righteousness, which the Lord, the righteous judge, shall give me at that day: and not to me only, but unto all them also that love his appearing" (2 Timothy 4:6-8).

What a contrast between the life of Solomon and that of Paul. What a difference between the lives of these two men. Let us compare these two men in the light of today, the hour in which we live.

The Life of Solomon

For quite a long season, Solomon was snared in the grip of pessimism. He was cynical, sarcastic, and in dark despair regarding his outlook on life. Immortality never entered his mind. He was living for the moment only.

Let me ask you a question: *Does that describe your view on life—are you living for today only?* We are citizens of this world for perhaps sixty or seventy years—some of us more, some of us less. But that isn't the end, for after this life on earth, we shall go to be citizens of another world forever and ever. I remind you that the doctrine of immortality is not a dead doctrine. You cannot close your mind or your ears to it and cause it to go away, for as surely as there is life there is also death. Solomon tried to close his mind to immortality, but it did not work for him and it will not work for you. Immortality is not some vague philosophy or a misty dream. The doctrine of immortality is a great and moral dynamic that lifts life to a high level and drives it to great ends.

So I ask you: *What is your attitude toward life today?* You may step from the stage of action before the week is over and be somewhere else before Saturday's midnight hour has struck. You and I have no guarantee of another tomorrow, no guarantee of another beat of our hearts. We are absolutely dependent upon Almighty God for each breath that we take into our bodies. In reality, we have only a few fleeting years, and then we leave this life that we know to go somewhere else forever and ever.

For years Solomon lived an utterly self-centered life. As we read his unfolding and remarkable story in the Old Testament, it would seem that he was among the most self-centered men of his day. He planned, he built, he acted with an eye to his own pleasure, to his own honor, and to his own ease. The Book of Ecclesiastes may be among the most pessimistic books of the Bible, as it tells of Solomon's terrible plight. But at its close, we read of Solomon's final recovery and his wise conclusion: "Let us hear the conclusion of the whole matter: Fear God, and keep his commandments: for this is the whole duty of man" (Ecclesiastes 12:13). This is what we should live for: *To fear God reverently and keep His commandments faithfully.*

If we look at Solomon's personal life, we see he tried everything.

He was well-educated and intelligent—the wisest man of his day. He was an explorer and a writer, one who searched near and far and delved into all avenues and sources for information. But after all was said and done, he came back and said, "Much study is a weariness of the flesh" (Ecclesiastes 12:12). I have read those words scores of times. Solomon spent his life devoted to pleasure, gave full reign to his five physical senses, looked upon all the evils and the pleasures that man can know in the world, and then concluded: "All is vanity and vexation of the spirit" (Ecclesiastes 2:17).

Solomon followed all the pleasures he could conceive. He had many wives, from all lands, of all faiths—yet he had to concede that all was vanity and vexation of spirit.

Then he tried power. He gathered wealth from all the ends of the great empires about him and formed for himself the outstanding kingdom of his day, a powerful army, and a vast retinue of servants—a mighty company that gave him applause, praise, and approbation and bowed down before him. He amassed power in all of its forms—wealth, rulership, kingship—yet he returned from it all and labeled it all vanity and vexation of spirit. His reaction to it all was to hate life, to loathe himself, and almost to consider it better never to have been born. He held in abomination all the power with which he had surrounded himself, and he looked back on his life with loathing.

This man of great ability, of tremendous power and of wisdom in a worldly sense, had missed the whole concept of the meaning and the mission of life. There are millions living today who breathe the same cry: "We have tried everything. We have tasted of power, tasted of pleasure, but we have found that in the end, all is vanity, all is empty. There is no real happiness or genuine satisfaction in all the forms of earthly power." America today needs to wake up before the currents of evil carry us even farther down the stream than we are now, and heaven knows we are too far already.

Finally, in Solomon's old age, he became conscious of the fact that he was a citizen of two worlds and it was then that he said: "Let us hear the conclusion of the whole matter: Fear God and keep his commandments: for this is the whole duty of man" (Ecclesiastes 12:13). What profound words! Solomon was recovered by the might of God before his day was done, and he gave forth great counsel before his sun was set.

The Life of Paul

Now let us look to Paul—who to me was the mightiest man of the New Testament and the greatest single credential that Christianity has had from the start of the Church age. His attitude toward life was far different from that of Solomon, as different as the east is from the west. I believe that Paul was among the most joyful people who ever lived, although his tribulations were overwhelming and he did not have an easy life.

In 2 Corinthians 11:24-27 Paul tells of his tribulations. He had been whipped five times, beaten with rods three times, once stoned, shipwrecked three times, imprisoned many times and: "In journeyings often, in perils of waters, in perils of robbers, in perils by mine own countrymen, in perils by the heathen, in perils in the city, in perils in the wilderness, in perils in the sea, in perils among false brethren; In weariness and painfulness, in watchings often, in hunger and thirst, in fastings often, in cold and nakedness." Paul went through it all, yet he came forth victoriously. He declared, "In all these things we are more than conquerors" (Romans 8:37), and he spoke those words with utter confidence and security. Why? He was secure in Christ and knew from whom he received his strength. He was not defeated on a single score. He had the right attitude toward life.

Again and again Paul was able to write the words, "Rejoice in the Lord alway: and again I say, Rejoice" (Philippians 4:4). Paul was irrepressible, unconquerable, joyful—a man who lived life to the fullest because he had a real purpose for living. Solomon said, "I hate life." Paul said, "I rejoice in Christ." Paul knew a full life that was yielded to God's perfect will.

Perhaps as never before you have become aware of how vastly important is your attitude toward life. You and I are eternity bound. *What are you living for?* My friend, we pass this way but once and we have but one life to live. Therefore, let us give our lives first to God, then following in Christ's footsteps and His example, give our lives to humanity and those about us, following God's perfect plan for our lives.

CHAPTER SEVEN

To Handle Difficulties

There is something that is very real to all of us who are a part of humanity, and that is the fact that there are troubles, there are sorrows, and there are difficulties that confront us all. Never think that because I am God's child and anointed of Him that I have no troubles, no problems or no difficulties. The reason that I can help you with your problems and your troubles and your sorrows is because I have troubles too, just like you do. If I didn't, I could never tell you what to do with yours, for we cannot give to anyone else more than we have experienced ourselves. I could not tell you what to do when you have a broken heart if my own heart had not been broken. I could not give you words of comfort if I had not gone through sorrow myself and been comforted by God, who is the God of all comfort. I can only give you what I know from personal experience about how to handle difficulties.

First of all, remember something: *A difficulty can break or make you.* When you come face to face with a difficulty in that life of yours, it will either make you a bigger, a stronger, a better person, or that difficulty will break you. It depends entirely on you—what you do with it. It does not depend on someone else, the person with whom you live, or the one with whom you are associated. It is natural to try to put the blame on someone else, instead of facing the problem and handling it the way you should. It all depends on how you take hold of it that spells out the results.

Sometimes I think that our difficulties can be compared to knives that either serve us or cut us. How we grasp them—by the blade or by the handle—determines whether we are cut or served. To take hold of a difficulty in the wrong way brings the same results as clutching a knife by the blade, and that's what some folks always seem to do. Perhaps a difficulty has come into your life and the first thing you did was grab it by the blade. It cut you, and it wasn't long before you found that the difficulty mastered you. You were hurt. You were defeated. But when you grasp your trouble by the handle, you can use it to your advantage, and it can become the greatest and most valuable tool that ever came into your life.

Difficulty is an inescapable fact of life, and Almighty God put it there for a purpose. We must never forget that it is God's purpose to make stronger men and women of us. God never created you or me to be weak or defeated. He made us to be strong people, and He could not make us strong without difficulty coming into our lives. So we should be thankful for difficulty. We should be proud that God deemed us able to handle the trouble. Many times I have looked up and said: "Dear Lord, if You didn't think I could take it, You wouldn't have permitted it. You have more confidence in me than I have in myself, so I will not focus my eyes on my own lack, but on Your faith in me. Thank You for the compliment."

If God could anoint your eyes with Holy Spirit eye salve, causing you to see why He allowed that difficulty to come into your life, then instead of tears of self-pity you would shed tears of joy, and you would be the happiest person in the world.

One of the nicest compliments that a human being can pay another is to say that person can deal with a difficult situation. Can you say that of yourself? Can I? How well do we handle difficulty? And how do we do it? It's one thing to talk about it, but it's another thing to look the trouble directly in the face and discern the answer as to how to cope with it.

First of all, start with the Word of God. That must be the basis of all things. The Holy Spirit exhorts us through the apostle Paul to say like him: "I can do all things through Christ which strengtheneth me" (Philippians 4:13). That portion of the Word of God has literally become a living and vital part of every moment of my day. It has done so much for me and for countless men and women everywhere. In our own power, unaided, we can be wholly lacking in strength and ineffective for the task, but when we draw our strength from Jesus Christ and live by Him, we are able to overcome our difficulties.

You may be asking how you can do all these things through Christ Jesus. Here is the secret. First of all, be quiet. When difficulty strikes, there is the human tendency to become anxious, frustrated, disturbed. We cannot handle difficulties well unless we are calm and composed. You must have your wits about you, able to think clearly, and you cannot when the surface of your mind is disturbed. The first essential therefore is to get quiet.

Go some place where you can be alone. Until recently I did not fully understand something that Jesus said: "When thou prayest, enter into thy closet, and when thou hast shut the door, pray to thy Father" (Matthew 6:6). The longer I live, the more I realize the power and the strength there is in prayerful quietness. That is why, in our services, I ask the congregation to be still before the Lord for one full minute. We are living in a generation of frustrated, jittery, and nervously tense people. *One of the secrets we must learn is that of being quiet before the LORD.*

In the face of trouble, therefore, instead of crying, go someplace alone and shut the door. All outer distractions should be reduced to a minimum, a place where you are not disturbed. As you enter into the presence of God, let go and listen to your mighty Creator, the One who is perfect wisdom and perfect knowledge. As He speaks, listen to Him. Receive instruction from Him.

Perhaps you have found that your nerves are torn by living in a world of chaos, worry, and confusion. But when you rest in His presence, He comes with the good news of His love, resources, and power. So as you put yourself at God's disposal, He cleanses, He makes whole, He brings healing, reinforcing all your weak places with His mighty strength.

"When thou prayest, enter into thy closet, and when thou hast shut the door, pray to thy Father." And as you do, you will find the reality of that glorious portion of the Word of God: *"I can do all things!"* You will not be overcome or defeated by anything that enters into your life. You can do all things through Christ who not only strengthens you but gives you wisdom, guidance, and help.

So when you come up against a difficulty and it looms mighty big compared to your strength, might, and wisdom, remember who you are by the grace of God and to whom you belong. Then ask God's help in stretching your mind to where it can handle that difficulty in Christ. If you will do it, no difficulty or problem will defeat you for one split second. Christ will see you through to glorious victory.

CHAPTER EIGHT

Waiting Upon the Lord

THEY THAT WAIT UPON THE LORD SHALL RENEW THEIR
STRENGTH; THEY SHALL MOUNT UP WITH WINGS AS
EAGLES; THEY SHALL RUN, AND NOT BE WEARY;
AND THEY SHALL WALK, AND NOT FAINT.
ISAIAH 40:31

Most of us have delighted to repeat this promise again and again as a comfort and a means of strength to our fainting hearts. But are we finding the blessings that are mentioned here to be common in our lives? Let's face it. Too many times I feel that we run and we are weary, we walk and we faint.

As we study these first six words carefully—"They that wait upon the LORD"—we see that we have just one condition to meet. That's all. It's very simple. But upon that single condition four glorious blessings hinge.

It is not impossible for any man or woman to meet that condition. It can be reached by all.

Notice that the second word after the condition is "shall." God has given the promise, and there is power and authority in His promises. Therefore, if we do not get results it proves that either we did not meet the condition or we do not understand its meaning. It's similar to this thing we call faith. I will admit to you that I get a bit impatient when someone comes before me and says, "Oh, Miss Kuhlman, I have all the faith in the world, and yet nothing happens."

Let me try to explain. From the Word of God I know that if any man or woman has even the smallest measure of faith, the results of that faith will be manifest. When someone insists he has "all the faith in the world" and yet nothing has happened, there is a reason for the stalemate. Either the condition has not been met, or that person has no genuine understanding of the real meaning of faith.

So it is with this glorious promise given to us by the LORD through the prophet Isaiah. If you are still running and are weary, if you are walking and are fainting, then either you have not met the condition or you do not understand the meaning of the promise.

"They that *wait* upon the LORD *shall*." The secret is found in that one condition—*waiting*. Before I go any further, let me point out that waiting and praying are different things. Prayer always precedes waiting, and the two—prayer and waiting—must go hand in hand. Sometimes I wonder just how much most folk know about praying, and I believe you will appreciate the following example and see my point.

When our missionary representative returned from a convention recently, he related an incident he had witnessed. About ten minutes before the speaker for the convention took his place on the platform to give his message, he slipped into the prayer room, where our representative was praying. No sooner had the speaker gone inside when a brother in the Lord came bursting through the doorway. This brother took off his coat, tossed it on a chair, put his Bible beside it, dropped to his knees, and then as loud as he could began to shout: "GLORY! GLORY! HALLELUJAH! GLORY TO GOD! AMEN! PRAISE GOD! GLORY!"

Perhaps you have had a similar experience and I need go no farther. He kept repeating the same phrases, and for about five minutes he disturbed everyone else in the prayer room who was really praying. Then just as quickly as he had come, he got up, dusted off the knees of his trousers, put on his coat, picked up his Bible, and left. When the door closed behind him, the speaker looked up and said, "Dear God, what did he say?"

When you pray, *say something*! Be specific and definite in your prayer. When you talk to God, talk to Him in the same way you would if you could literally see Him. If you have a need, express it. That, my friend, is true prayer.

Waiting on the Lord, however, is not the same as prayer. Waiting—a condition of this glorious promise—means to be silent, to be still, saying nothing. You and I will agree that we are living in an age of intense activity. This is an age of noise. Some people turn on their radio the minute they wake up in the morning and never turn it off until they go to bed at night. There are those who admit they cannot sleep unless they keep the radio on throughout the night. Pure silence disturbs their sleep. There are others who turn on the television set the very second they get up in the morning. They may not watch or really listen all day long, but they never turn it off again until they retire at night.

You may have already guessed the reason for these observations. This age of noise and intense activity has so saturated our beings that even our souls have become noisy. It is the hardest thing in the world for people today to get to the place where they are quiet before the Lord. We all find it difficult to be still in the presence of the Lord. Yet the Scripture admonishes us, "Be still, and know that I am God" (Psalm 46:10).

The other day I saw a little grandmother sitting with her hands relaxed in her lap, slowly turning her thumbs, one over the other. I stopped dead in my tracks, awed by this sight. My grandmother used to do this, but not grandmothers or mothers today. Few of them ever get that relaxed anymore.

Now after you have prayed, be still, be silent, be quiet; but in that time of waiting, be filled with expectancy and hope. The Psalmist said, "My expectation is from him" (Psalm 62:5). In your waiting before the Lord, you are not waiting as an idler or one who is lazy. No, beloved. In those hours of waiting and silence, there is an expectancy. You prayed, and you prayed believing. Now you are in that state of waiting with great expectancy for Him to do that which you have asked in faith believing.

Chapter Nine

Peace of Mind

There is something that I feel is mighty important. It's something for which I am very grateful, but it is also something that I realize is lacking in the lives of thousands and thousands of people today. That something is *peace of mind.*

There are comparatively few people who have honest-to-goodness peace of mind—who can go home after a day's work, lie down and without a sedative or a sleeping pill, go to sleep and then sleep all night without being disturbed by some kind of mental torment. Peace of mind is the most important possession an individual can know outside of his own salvation. Even if a person enjoys health, beauty, talent, power, love, fame, money and prestige and lacks peace of mind, his life is a hideous torment and an intolerable burden.

There are several basic reasons why so many people do not have this blessed inner peace, and I am going to be very practical with you about the whole thing. As Papa used to say, "I'm not going to spare the horses."

First of all, I want to touch on something that is very present in most lives. Too many of us worry about the things we do not have, and then we become dissatisfied with what we do have. From my personal observations, I believe this is one of the most discontented generations that ever existed. Let me give you an example. I remember an old Missourian who lived in the Ozarks where the country is beautiful and the scenery is gorgeous. As he was talking to me, he spoke about the days when he and his family had very little. His folks were poor. His relatives were poor. The neighbors were all poor. But they were happy poor people. There was little dissatisfaction among them and they rarely complained. They enjoyed their corn bread and black-eyed peas. In the summer time, the children went barefoot and didn't worry about shoes until school resumed in the fall. He said they were all so contented and happy.

That is, until the day the mail carrier left a mail order catalog at a neighbor's house. That did it! Nobody was happy or contented after that. It disrupted the neighbor's family, his family, the families of the in-laws—even the out-laws were unhappy. Everything was serene until that day.

Everybody in the neighborhood began looking at the catalog, first wonderingly, then longingly, and then it seemed that nobody was satisfied from that day on. Soon the people forgot the beauty of the lakes and the trees that surrounded them. Instead of sitting outdoors in the evening, marveling at God's wonders in the heavens, they stayed indoors, burning their kerosene lamps, leafing through the mail order catalogs, making themselves miserable at the thought of the many things they did not possess. He said, "My wife began nagging me. The kids began begging for things. It was never the same again, and we never had real peace and contentment at our house after that."

As I was going down the street the other day, I chanced on a scene that I'm sure is familiar to you. There was a mother pulling her screaming youngster out of a toy store. I stopped, thinking he must be in great pain. Then I noticed something. He was clutching a small toy in his hand, and perhaps you can guess the rest of my story and the reason why that child was screaming and kicking the way he was. He was miserable because he couldn't have all the other toys he had seen in the store. He wasn't satisfied with the cute little toy car that his mother had just purchased for him.

Yes, it's like that. Had the mother brought a little toy home to him, he would have been thrilled with it, loved it, and played with it, for hours or days. But because he had seen all the other toys that he could *not* have, he was unhappy and miserable.

That's human nature! We need to be practical about some of these things, to use our good common sense. Someone asked a noted bishop the secret of his serene spirit, and he replied: "As I grow older, life becomes simpler and more peaceful because I see the essentials more clearly in the evening light of my life."

His remark brings my Mama to mind. You know, when I was a youngster, we had a crisis at our house at least once every two years, and it got so that I looked forward to it—and I think Papa did, too. Papa knew when to expect it, and do you know why? Because it came every time our furniture company in Concordia received a new type of china closet. How Mama just loved her china—she loved it because Aunt Belle would order the closet from France and Aunt Belle also painted china. As a result, she and Mama had some of the finest china in Missouri. Mama thought a lot of her china, and so she doted on china closets. Every time there was a new model, Mama started on Papa—easy at first—but it wasn't long before she was nagging him. There was no peace until Mama had the new model from the furniture store where they always stocked the biggest and the best, because they knew that Joe Kuhlman would have to buy it for Mrs. Kuhlman.

But like the bishop whose statement I quoted earlier, in Mama's later years of life, she never even looked at china closets. Buffets didn't mean anything to her. Even her beautiful china didn't mean too much. It meant far more to her to have my brother come home, to sit down by her side on the sofa, and talk with her for an hour or so. That meant more to Mama than all the china closets in the world.

Now this is my point. It is wisdom to learn not to make a crisis situation out of every unhappy experience and out of everything that we want and cannot have. Are your crises making everybody around you miserable? These things that appear so important are not the essential things. It is far more essential that you have peace of soul, for after you have peace of soul you will have peace of mind. Otherwise, if you are not careful, before long you will develop a crisis psychology, and every situation will bring a crisis to your door.

We are a part of the human race, and there will be sickness, financial difficulties, conflicts with the children and the other members of the family, or one of a thousand other things. We all experience crises, and if we are not careful it won't be long until we find that our outer conflicts are destroying our inner peace.

There are also conflicts between ourselves and other people that destroy our peace. Our feelings are hurt or we carry a grudge. You will never have peace of mind so long as there is a grievance, or a grudge, or an unforgiving spirit in your heart. The other person may know nothing about it, but while you carry a grievance in your own heart you will never have peace in your mind. Your mind will never be peaceful until your heart is peaceful. There is a Scripture that is marvelous. It is Isaiah 26:3—"Thou wilt keep him in perfect peace, whose mind is stayed on thee." Why? "Because he trusteth in thee."

Did you know that the mind rules the body? In fact, the world in which a man lives is created out of his own thoughts. The kind of world that you live in is created out of your own thoughts. God knew well the product of His creation. He knew that if His children put perfect trust and confidence in Him, their mind stayed on Him, resting in His faithfulness, then perfect peace could be theirs, knowing that He would take care of every problem, every need, and every tomorrow.

If in this moment God can get you to commit yourself completely to Him—your thoughts and the world which you have created for yourself, commit this moment to Him, commit yourself and all of your problems to

Him—then He will keep you in perfect peace, for your mind is stayed on Him.

What is the center of your thoughts? What governs your mind? You tell me the answer and I will tell you what governs you. Is there greed? Is there jealousy? Are you being mastered by other wrong desires? If your answer is "yes," then you are one of the unhappiest people that lives and breathes.

If you want real peace—peace of mind—then here is the formula: *God will keep you in perfect peace when your mind is anchored and stayed on Him, for He is the One who has all power to give peace of mind and peace of soul.*

CHAPTER TEN

Walk Uprightly

FATHER, THAT SOMEBODY A LITTLE DISCOURAGED,
CARRYING AN ESPECIALLY HEAVY BURDEN THIS HOUR,
THOSE WHO ARE GOING THROUGH THE DEEP WATERS, BE
THEIR STRENGTHENER. MAY THEY FEEL THE STRONG ARMS
OF CHRIST HOLDING THEM CLOSE TO YOUR GREAT HEART.
GIVE FAITH WHERE FAITH IS NEEDED, AND THAT EXTRA
STRENGTH TO TAKE EACH ONE THROUGH TO VICTORY.
AMEN.

You know, Jesus Christ has a way of making people believe two things about themselves. First, I am not what I ought to be. Second, I need not stay the way I am. In every one of us there is the mixture of the best and the worst, and it's just like that.

When I was a little girl, had you gone to Joe Kuhlman and asked him about his little red-haired, freckle-faced daughter, he would have told you that he was the proud possessor of the most perfect child ever born. You could never argue that with Joe Kuhlman. He had the perfect child in that red-haired, freckle-faced girl, and he might have told you how I insisted on doing the dishes when I was so little that Mama had to lower the oven door, and how Mama would place the dishpan on that oven door so I could do the dishes. Of course, Papa didn't tell you that was usually just before Christmas when I could imagine that Santa Claus was watching me through the window.

Or Joe Kuhlman might have told you what a generous little thing his red-haired girl was. To prove it he would tell you that while Mama attended a Methodist State Convention out of town, his six-year-old girl made iced tea for the whole neighborhood in Concordia, Missouri, delivering it to their back doors in gallon buckets, with Mama's compliments. Poor Mama didn't know one thing about it, and the Lord knows that none of the neighbors wanted that iced tea. But that was Papa's "wonderful girl!"

What Papa didn't tell you was about the time that this same "wonderful red-haired girl" of his, at the very height of the watermelon season, plugged all of Grandpa's wonderful watermelons. No sir! Papa would never tell you that about his girl. What was it? The best and the worst in one kid, and I was that kid!

I still must confess that I'm not all good. Neither are you. I have never met the person who was a perfect individual. I have never met the person who was all good because we are a strange combination of good and bad, and every human heart is an unseen battlefield where the good and the bad are fighting it out. Sometimes one side wins, and sometimes the other gains the victory.

When the bad wins out, we are ashamed and disgusted with ourselves. When the good wins, we have a clean feeling inside and we are filled with joy. We have proven ourselves to be a real person.

But do you want to know something? This being good only part of the time isn't good enough, and it isn't sufficient in the sight of God. It is as inconsistent as the way some people keep Lent. Throughout that holy season they won't drink one drop of liquor, but as soon as Lent is over they go back to their drinking. Others won't touch a cigarette for forty days, but as soon as Lent is over they smoke their heads off. There is no consistency in their thinking or their actions.

There is a promise in the Bible that is one of the greatest in the Word of God. If you want a guarantee for successful living, and assurance for security, here it is: Psalm 84:11— "No good thing will he [God] withhold from them that walk uprightly."

Recently I had occasion to talk with a fine Christian businessman who told me of speaking to a group of college students . Before his lecture began, he asked many of them what they desired most in looking for a position, what they desired more than anything else in life. All gave the same answer, summed up in one word: *security*. That's right, security.

God has guaranteed security for every person who will meet the condition: "to them that walk uprightly." Some folks never get a grip on success because there are too many other things they won't let go of. They cling to wrong ideas, wrong attitudes, wrong approaches, wrong associates, and wrong ways of living. In order to have security, in order to make life a success, you must get hold of the truth, and the Bible tells the truth. The Bible states, "No good thing will he withhold from them that walk uprightly."

Now what does it mean to walk uprightly? What does it consist of? It is when you know what is right and what is wrong, and you hold to what is right. You cannot fail to go right and achieve good things by thinking right and acting right. By the same token you can never go right by doing wrong. *Never.* Nobody in this world ever goes wrong who did not first think wrong. Think the right thing and you will do the right thing, and you will get the right results. It works. It is a known fact that a thought makes a deed, a deed makes a life, and a life makes a destiny. *The important technique for having things turn out right is to start right—and you start right by thinking right.*

I feel there is also something further intended by this statement that the Lord will not withhold any good thing from a person who walks uprightly. "Uprightly" means to walk in right ways. It means being strong. God did not create us to be a defeated people. I do not believe for one single moment that God's plan for your life was one of defeat. Oh, I know the opposition you face is strong. I know what the forces of unrighteousness are like. I am a part of humanity too, but I also know the secret of living an undefeated life. The Master has made provision for it, and it's found in Ephesians 6:10-17.

Finally, my brethren, be strong in the Lord, and in the power of his might.

Put on the whole armour of God, that ye may be able to stand against the wiles of the devil.

For we wrestle not against flesh and blood, but against principalities, against powers, against the rulers of the darkness of this world, against spiritual wickedness in high places.

Wherefore take unto you the whole armour of God, that ye may be able to withstand in the evil day, and having done all, to stand.

Stand therefore, having your loins girt about with truth, and having on the breastplate of righteousness;

And your feet shod with the preparation of the gospel of peace;

Above all, taking the shield of faith, wherewith ye shall be able to quench all the fiery darts of the wicked.

And take the helmet of salvation, and the sword of the Spirit, which is the word of God.

The Lord has given us glorious weapons to assure our success. Look at the marvelous pieces of armor that He has provided. Truth is our girdle, sincerity in the inward parts. Righteousness our breastplate, sheltering the heart. Shoes defend the feet against sharp sticks, stones, and bruises, and when our feet are shod with the gospel of peace, we walk with a steady pace regardless of what comes into our lives, or what happens to us.

There is no substitute for the shield of faith: "this is the victory that overcometh the world, even our faith" (1 John 5:4). Be fully persuaded of the truth of God's promises and you will never be defeated. The helmet of salvation protects and secures the head with sanctified wisdom and knowledge. Next comes the sword of the Spirit, the Word of God.

Then comes the secret of strength. "Finally, my brethren, be strong." Strong in your own strength? No! Through your own willpower? No! "Be strong in the Lord, and in the power of His might." *There is the secret of strength.*

Now let us go back to the promise in Psalm 84: "No good thing will he withhold from them that walk uprightly," which means those who are clean, those who are strong. You may accept the truth of what I am saying, but you may also be thinking, "I wish I was like that, but I'm not clean. Neither am I strong."

Now the person who admits he is neither clean nor strong thereby opens himself to the grace of God, and the grace of God is the power that can change a man or woman and make that person clean and strong. Even in strength we do not achieve great things without God's help. The grace of God through our Lord Jesus Christ can utterly change a person. It can change you no matter how mixed up or how messed up you are this hour. Christ can change you. Christ can make you clean and can make you strong. But it requires a price.

Do you remember what I said at the beginning of this message, that some people never get a grip on success because there are too many other things they won't let go of? Well, if you want real success, you have to go all out. Not just during the forty-day Lenten period. Not only on Sundays, but all out every day of every week. You must give God all that you are. You have to surrender. You can't hold anything back. He will give to you as you give yourself to Him. And if you really surrender to Him, He will change you.

What happens then? You will begin getting what you want out of life. You will have security, and I promise you that God's guarantee for security is the greatest I know anything about. You will have peace of mind as a result. You will be blessed—and to have the blessing of God prompts me to ask, "What more is there to desire?" Situations will begin turning out right for you, your problems will be solved, for you have God's promise and His guarantee when you have met the condition. *"No good thing will he withhold from them that walk uprightly."*

CHAPTER ELEVEN

Victories Are Cheap That Come Cheap

I received a letter from a woman who chanced to tune in one of my radio programs. For more than four years she has cared for her ailing father, who was a consecrated and godly man, having served in the pulpit most of his life. Now the daughter is having a running battle with massive self-pity. As a result, her life is a total wreckage, stripped of value, and her heart is filled with questions about ultimates—what purpose there is in anything. All she can feel is a great aching void and emptiness, and a sense of futility about almost everything. She asked me the question, "What can I do?"

My first reaction to this woman's question was this: *Does she actually believe what her father taught and preached for more than sixty years?* If her father preached the truth, if she believed what he preached, then she need not be living a life of defeat, for there is victory in the Lord Jesus Christ.

God's Word in Philippians 4:13 states, "I can do all things through Christ which strengtheneth me." And God's Word cannot and will not fail. Know that! *I can do all things. You can do all things.* No man or woman need ever be defeated, and this daughter, whose letter touched my heart so deeply, need know no defeat whatsoever unless she consents to be defeated. Her father preached it. He believed it. Does she believe the Word of God? If she will believe it, she will do something about it. She is going to act like it and she will gain the victory.

First of all, I'm going to say something that you may not have considered before. The writer of this letter is perhaps waiting for some miracle to happen on the outside. It is a mistake for any of us to wait for some miracle to be performed from without, lifting us above our self-centeredness, above our fears and doubts. A person helps God from within by turning with outgoing love to others, and then miraculously all fears, doubts, and self-centeredness vanish. But not until then. The miracle starts from within and not from without. You must throw your will on the side of outgoing love, and all the healing resources of the universe will be behind you.

Neither God nor man, however, can help you if you remain bottled up in yourself, in your own self-pity, and in your own self-centeredness. All the medicine that you can take, all the advice that I might be able to give you, all the sermons you may hear, everything that you might know mentally, will never help you until you start doing something yourself. Neither God nor anyone else can help you if you remain closed up in your own self-pity. I urge you to get out of yourself or you will perish. Get out of yourself or you will remain a defeated person.

Do you want to know something? I have learned that victories that come cheap are cheap. Only those are worth having that come as a result of hard fighting, and sometimes the fighting becomes mighty hard and relentless. But those are the victories that are worthwhile victories. I know from personal experience that this is so. It was the stones that bruised my feet that made me strong. It was the Gethsemanes in my life, those hard battles and testing times when I felt I was almost crushed and the waters almost overflowed, that fashioned the qualities of courage and trust deep within me. Those victories that came easily were worth little. But there will never be a dungeon in your life where the Master is not able and willing to give you grace and victory in your darkest hour.

Think with me for a moment. Did you know that Milton wrote *Paradise Lost* when blind? He did not allow affliction to rob him of the victory. Then there was a man who was set aside with a broken hip, and while lying in bed, continually looking at the wallpaper around him, he conceived the idea of becoming a sketch artist, and became a very successful one. He, too, found grace in his darkest hour. These two men could have been defeated in their dungeon, but they gained the victory.

A poet failed miserably on his first night of a public reading, and felt the scornful shame of his audience laughing at him. But instead of accepting defeat, he went home and wrote his greatest inspirational work on the ability to *take it* in spite of failure. His poem came to the attention of a man hospitalized, one who had lost both arms and feet. He was so inspired that he became a successful public reader. Yes, all of these found grace in their dungeons.

I once learned of a doctor who was totally paralyzed in her lower limbs as a result of infantile paralysis. When she applied for acceptance at medical colleges here in America, they refused her, saying she could never practice medicine in her condition. Was she defeated? Not on your life. No one can disagree that she had reason to be defeated and discouraged, but this is what she did. She went to China and received her medical degree there, where she stood at the top of her class. Not only that, she returned to one of the very cities where she had been refused acceptance at their medical college, passed her state exam, and is now practicing medicine from her wheelchair in an institution for handicapped children.

No man or woman need ever be defeated on a single score unless they consent to be defeated. You may lose both feet and yet there is victory. You may lose both arms and yet there is victory. You may lose the sight of your eyes, or the hearing in both ears, and yet there is victory. *Victories that come cheap are cheap.* Only those that come as a result of hard fighting are worth having. *The rose-strewn paths the weaklings creep, but brave hearts dare to climb the steep.*

Holy Father:
Give us courage,
Give us faith;
Give us victory,
For Jesus' sake!